The Adventures of CAPTAIN CARROT & BRAVE BROCCOLI

JOURNEY TO THE STARS

Daniel Chimes

The Adventures of Captain Carrot & Brave Broccoli: Journey to the Stars
ISBN: 978-1-8384983-1-3

First published in Great Britain
in 2021 through Amazon self-publishing
service Kindle Direct Publishing

Produced in the UK by The Book Writers' Resource
tbwr.co.uk

Copyright © Daniel Chimes

Daniel Chimes has asserted his right under the Copyright, Design and Patents
Act 1988 to be identified as the author of this work.

Disclaimer:
This book is sold subject to the condition that it shall not, by way of trade or
otherwise, be lent, resold, hired out, or otherwise circulated without the author's
prior consent in any form of binding or cover and without a similar condition,
including this condition, being imposed on the subsequent publisher.

To my girls—thank you for motivating
me to embark on this journey
To all the children—keep reading, keep
learning and keep adventuring

Standing high up in the Mountains on a warm summer night,
Captain Carrot and Brave Broccoli saw a captivating **sight**.
As far as they could see were a million tiny stars,
Floating through the heavens like little candles in little jars.

"I wonder what it's like up there" Captain Carrot said out loud.
"I wish that we could go ourselves, but I don't think it's allowed!"
Why not?" Brave Broccoli asked, "Who says that we can't go?"
"If we make a plan and work real hard, who can tell us no?"

So our heroes started to build a ship to fly to space
But rocket science is really hard and nothing fell in place.
"This is too tricky" they said, "We'll never get it done!"
"I guess we're meant to stay on Earth and not go chase the Sun!"

But a Wise Old Badger peeked his head up over the fence,
"It seems to me all you need is a bit of **confidence!**"
"The greatest things are hard, so please do not forget -
"If you build the skills you need in life, any challenge can be met."

With new determination they studied how to make a rocket,
Learning every widget, every gadget, every electric socket.
Using these skills they started to build, with tools in their grip,
Confident that with real hard work they'd build a rocketship.

After weeks and months of working, everything was in place
For them to climb aboard their ship and fly off into space!
The countdown started and the engines made an incredible sound
And in the blink of an eye they were flying off the ground.

The Earth's beauty took their breath when they went for a look,
It was far more beautiful than anything they'd seen in any book.
Their journey to the stars began, there was no turning back
And so they gave a final wave and got themselves on track.

Meanwhile, very far away, another quest had begun,
Zargos the Alien left her world in a spacecraft built for one.
Like our heroes, Zargos dreamt of discovering planets new,
And so she hopped into her ship and towards the stars she flew.

Captain Carrot and Brave Broccoli travelled at full speed,
Looking to find brand new worlds and excited to proceed.
They saw something red and green, and both their hearts soared;
Before them was a **great big planet** waiting to be explored!

They worked together to safely bring the ship to the ground,
They jumped out, stretched their legs and took a look around.
Brave Broccoli spotted something far off and down below,
"Another traveller," he cried aloud. "We must go say hello!"

"Greetings" said Brave Broccoli, "we've just come to this place!"
"Do you live upon this planet? Or have you come from outer space?"
"I come from far away," she said, "it's good to see you here!"
"I'm exploring this planet too, but my ship is broken, I fear!"

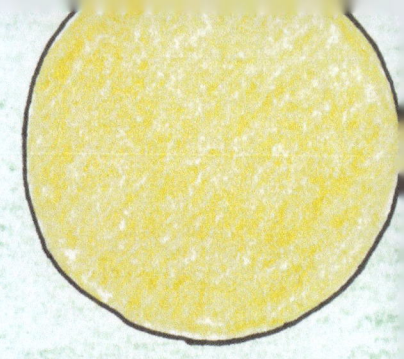

"No need to fear" our heroes cried, "We know just what to do!"
"If you need a hand to fix your ship, we will happily help you!"
And so the three set to work, mending every part,
Turning a wrench, swinging a hammer, working hard and smart.

After hours of toiling away they wondered, "**will it fly?**"
Zargos jumped into the seat and gave the starter a try.
It lifted up above the ground and they all said, "that went well!"
"All we needed was a bit of knowledge and belief in ourselves!"

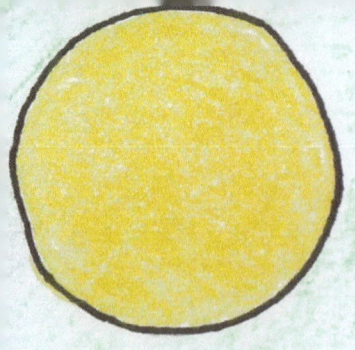

"Thank you both," Zargos said, "for getting me on track!
"It has been great to meet you two, but I must be getting back.
"Please take this gift back home with you, a map of the stars,
"It will help you find your way through space, no matter near or far!"

They waved goodbye and then went back, ready to explore.
This red planet had much to see and they wanted to know more.
There were many wonderful things like nothing they'd ever seen,
Like trees that grew with purple leaves and an Ocean that was green!

After weeks of looking around they finally had their fill,
They made their way back to their ship standing on a hill.

The rocket blasted up again, climbing into the sky,
As they flew back into space they turned and said, "goodbye!"

They were ready to return to Earth after finding great new things,
They'd seen many stars, many moons and planets with big rings!
But now they wanted to see their home and take a little rest
And think about the things they'd learned from going on this quest.

They had made a friend from outer space and helped her on her way,
They had seen things more beautiful than any words can say.
They had been given a map of space with pride of place on their shelves,
But most important, they had learned to be **confident** in themselves.

Titles by this author

Captain Carrot & Brave Broccoli:
Escape from Rabbit Island

Captain Carrot & Brave Broccoli:
Journey to the Stars

Printed in Great Britain
by Amazon